IMAGES
of America

BELMAR

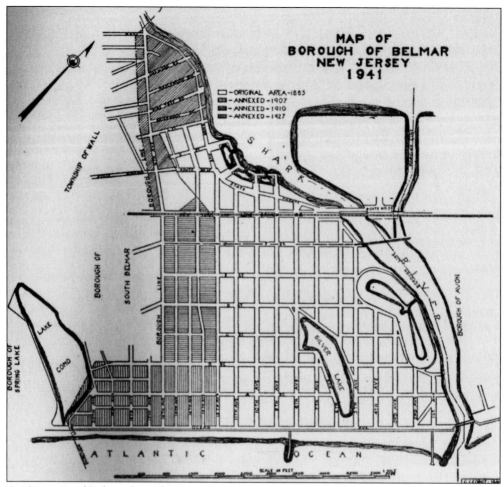

A 1941 map of Belmar from the Inventory of the Municipal Archives of New Jersey, prepared by the Historical Records Survey Work Projects Administration (WPA), clearly illustrates the expansion of the borough as indicated by the various shadings.

IMAGES
of America

BELMAR

Karen L. Schnitzspahn

ARCADIA

First published 1997
Copyright © Karen L. Schnitzspahn, 1997

ISBN 0-7524-0841-0

Published by Arcadia Publishing,
an imprint of the Chalford Publishing Corporation,
One Washington Center, Dover, New Hampshire 03820.
Printed in Great Britain

Library of Congress Cataloging-in-Publication Data applied for

This book is dedicated to
Lois T. Gallagher

She runs the Belmar Public Library
Always wearing a smile.
Attractive, charming, and
Interested in others,
Intelligent and resourceful.
Her contributions to the
Community of Belmar,
Over the years,
Are too numerous to list.
Lois Gallagher is a gem.
May all the luck in the world
Come her way!

Contents

Acknowledgments

Many people contributed photographs, information, and enthusiasm to help me prepare this book. They are all so wonderful! I appreciate each and every one of them. This awesome task was made pleasant by having the opportunity to meet many "Belmarians" and others with an interest in Belmar while I was researching.

Thank you to the Belmar Public Library, Lois T. Gallagher (to whom I dedicate this book), and Grace T. Roper, who wrote the first book on Belmar. I am especially grateful to Dennis Lewis for sharing photographs and knowledge about the town's history, and to the Belmar Historical Council. My sincere thanks to Mayor Kenneth E. Pringle, The Belmar Tourism Development Commission, and especially Sharon K. Day and Patricia O'Keefe. Also, I would like to thank John Szeliga, The Belmar Environmental Commission, and The Shark River Environmental Roundtable.

Special recognition and deepest appreciation go to the following people who not only loaned photographs but also took great interest in this project: Claire Angrist, Mildred Desmond Day, Sandra Epstein, Irene and Pat McCann Jr., Pat McCann III, Robert V. and Lorraine Pringle, John A. and Dorothy Taylor, and John Walsifer.

Very special thanks to Glenn Pringle of the Goodwill Hose Co. No. 1, Nick Mihalic and Ed Vetrecin of the Union Fire Co. No. 1, and Garry Young of the Volunteer Hook and Ladder Company. My heartfelt thanks to Frank Mihlon Jr. for sharing his memories and photographs about the origins of the Belmar First Aid Squad and his family history.

I would like to thank Fred Sigrist and Tom Gallagher of the Belmar Fishing Club for their help and their kindness. Also, a special thank you to Shay Blum of Birdsall Engineering, Inc., Dick Napoliton of Wall Township, Richard Riegler who runs the Belmar website on the Internet, and Janine Bilotti of *The Coast Star*.

Thank you to the following people who have each helped in individual ways; I appreciate your contributions: Shirley Carroll, Ruth Conklin, Raymond F. Davis, Jane Haulenbeek, Maria Hernandez, James Keenan, Jim Klug, Laurie McEvoy, Richard Neral, Richard Sherman, Harold Solomon, Virginia M. Slusser, and Robert L. White.

I give special recognition to my dear friends and esteemed colleagues in history who have been so supportive and helpful to me, not only with this book, but always. My heartfelt thanks go to Randall Gabrielan, Timothy J. McMahon, and George H. Moss Jr.

And last, but not least, of course is my family. I would like to thank my husband, Leon, and our sons, Doug and Greg. Their love and support gives me the strength and inspiration to keep going.

Karen L. Schnitzspahn
June 23, 1997

Introduction

"Beautiful Belmar is not a meaningless slogan. It is a fact attested to by its many distinctive features, among them: The coolest and balmiest seashore town along the North Jersey coast in summer. A mild, bracing temperature the rest of the year. Free from mosquitos. Within an hour and a half's train ride of the metropolis, with more than a hundred trains a day. One unbroken mile of clean, spacious beach, the safest for bathing on the whole Atlantic coast. Situated in the center of a wide stretch of boardwalk extending from Asbury Park to Sea Girt, a distance of six miles. An ocean boulevard wide enough for the passage of four cars and ample parking space; smooth as a billiard table, with the most open view of the Atlantic along the drive from Sandy Hook to Cape May. Two beautiful lakes."

The description above appeared in The Borough of Belmar's "Handy Guide" from 1929. Much of that booklet still holds true today. The beach and lakes, of course, haven't moved. However, there have also been many changes. Gradually, the large old hotels from the early 1900s either burned down or were demolished, and smaller guesthouses became popular, a trend that continues today. There may be fewer trains per day, but roads have improved. Buhler's Pavilion and picnic grove on the Shark River gave way to the big Belmar Marina in the 1930s. Fierce storms pounded Belmar over the years, but the town recovered well from them every time. Belmar's businesses, community services, and residential areas continue to thrive.

The 1997 promotional material calls Belmar "one of the Northeast's premier resorts" and that it is. For Belmar continues to survive as a resort after its founding 125 years ago. Belmar's current year-round population of around seven thousand swells to as much as sixty thousand in the summertime. The borough has experienced its share of difficulties, like any other resort town, but the strength of its people and a year-round sense of community have kept it alive.

This book does not attempt to cover the entire history of Belmar, for that would be impossible to do in one volume. A pictorial sampler of the town's background is presented, based upon the photographs and postcards that were made available to this author. This volume begins with images from the 1880s, a time when photography was becoming increasingly popular with hobbyists and tourists. The postcard craze of the early 1900s also provides many good views of Belmar. The images in each chapter are mainly from the first half of the twentieth century.

A brief overview of Belmar's early history and development may be of interest to readers. Most likely, the first people in the Belmar area were Lenape Indians who probably enjoyed many of the same things that visitors still do today, such as swimming, fishing, and crabbing. They called the Shark River the Nolletquesset. The river has a rich history and folklore legacy that are currently being documented in a video produced by the Shark River Environmental Roundtable.

Settled by Europeans around 1700, the area that is now Belmar began as part of Wall

Township with a small fishing and farming trade. Most of the farmland belonged to Peter White and other farmers including Newman, Bennett, and Brown. During the Revolutionary War, Belmar was known for its salt works, located near the F Street Bridge area. Salt was of importance to the Continental Army for preserving foods, and the salt works were targets for the British troops. The town's origin as an organized resort started in 1872, after the Civil War and during the period of Reconstruction. Religious camp meetings were popular and in 1869 the Methodists founded the resort of Ocean Grove. In 1872, a group of twenty-five businessmen from New York and Philadelphia who felt that Ocean Grove was getting too crowded decided to start a new community just 3 miles south and call it Ocean Beach. Mr. Abraham Bitner was appointed purchasing agent for the group. The membership rapidly grew to forty-one people, each of whom bought the first sixty shares of stock at $500 each. The Ocean Beach Association was incorporated by an act of the New Jersey Legislature on March 13, 1873. Bitner purchased the settlers' farms in 1872. Most of these rural properties were on the Manasquan Road (now F Street). The Ocean Beach Association planned the town beautifully with twelve wide streets all running from the Atlantic Ocean to the Shark River to provide free circulation of air, an appealing feature that sold many lots in the days before air conditioning.

In 1889, a heated issue of concern to property owners and summer residents of Ocean Beach was their desire for a more distinctive name for the town. People suggested a variety of names—"Wallmere" was a favorite. Surprisingly, the name "City of Elcho" won in an election, and yet that designation only lasted a month. A prominent land developer and resident of Ocean Beach, Henry Yard, who was bitter over losing some lawsuits against the town, instigated that name. Fortunately, Yard's wife came up with the idea of calling the town "Belmar" (French for "beautiful sea") and it became the official name on May 14, 1889.

Today, Belmar, located by the "beautiful sea" and the Shark River, offers both summer fun and good year-round living. Although not a resident of Belmar, I love visiting the town with its many attractions and friendly people. I have truly enjoyed compiling this book. As stated previously, however, there is so much more to cover about Belmar. With limitations of time and space, I did my best to include a well-rounded look at the town's history in pictures but there is surely much that was not included and rightfully should be. Hopefully, a second volume can fill in the gaps. Anyone who has photographs, information, or comments to contribute is welcome to write to the author at the following address: Karen L. Schnitzspahn, P.O. Box 716, Red Bank, NJ 07701. Meanwhile, relax on the beach in summer, or curl up in front of the fireplace in winter, and enjoy *Belmar*.

For Further Reading:
Belmar in Retrospect by Grace Trott Roper, originally published in 1978. This book, the first complete text about Belmar, was a monumental feat, for Mrs. Roper spent over ten years researching, compiling, and writing it. Mrs. Roper, a talented and gracious lady who ran the Belmar Public Library for years, is to be commended for her many achievements.

Belmar.com:
Belmar has a website on the internet. Be sure to visit http://www.belmar.com for information about the town, places to go, schedules of events, and features in the Belmar Online Magazine about history and interesting people.

One

When Belmar Was
Ocean Beach

A rare 1886 Ocean Beach album of photographs taken by Isaac Henderson reveals fascinating views of the northeastern section of what is now Belmar. This house was on the corner of Second Avenue and A Street. Henderson, a talented amateur photographer, owned a summer estate in Ocean Beach on Second Avenue. (Collection of Dennis Lewis.)

This Isaac Henderson image was taken from an upper porch on Second Avenue, looking east toward the ocean. The original Buena Vista Hotel is the building in the middle, and the house on the corner that still stands is easily recognized by its tower. (Collection of Dennis Lewis.)

From an upper porch, Isaac Henderson took this photograph of Ocean Beach, looking south. The Woodbine Cottage is on the right. In the distance can be seen the Episcopal church. Notice how much undeveloped land still existed in 1886. (Collection of Dennis Lewis.)

In this Henderson photograph, facing north, the Buckingham Hotel in Key East (now Avon-by-the-Sea) can be seen to the right across the Shark River. The Buckingham was in existence until recently when it was torn down. (Collection of Dennis Lewis.)

The gingerbread porch trim and the gentleman relaxing in a rocking chair enhance the charm of this Isaac Henderson 1886 album photograph, looking west on Second Avenue. The railroad bridge over the Shark River is barely visible in the distance. (Collection of Dennis Lewis.)

Isaac Henderson photographed "The Point," including the Columbia Hotel on Ocean Avenue and buildings silhouetted on Second Avenue, from a sandbar in the Shark River in 1886. (Collection of Dennis Lewis.)

This delightful image of fun-loving children enjoying a boat on the Shark River is a detail from a larger Isaac Henderson photograph. The date is August 23, 1886. (Collection of Dennis Lewis.)

On November 24, 1885, high winds and angry waves ravaged the *Malta*, a full-rigged iron vessel sailing from Antwerp to New York, leaving the ship wrecked at Ocean Beach near the foot of Ninth Avenue. Local lifesaving crews made heroic efforts and rescued the *Malta*'s crew using a breeches buoy, but one of the ship's sailors drowned. (Laurie McEvoy.)

Dex, Marion, and Malcolm, playing on the sand at Ocean Beach, look toward their father Isaac Henderson as he captures their youthful exuberance with his lens (detail of a larger 1886 photograph). In the distance on the right, the beached wreck of the *Malta* is faintly visible in the original print of the photograph. (Collection of Dennis Lewis.)

The 1889 *Wolverton Atlas of Monmouth County*'s map of Ocean Beach shows the original town as laid out by the Ocean Beach Association. The name was changed to Belmar that same year, probably much to the mapmaker's dismay. Lots belonging to the Ocean Beach Association are marked "O.B.A." There are "hot and cold water baths" at the site of the Fifth Avenue Pavilion.

14

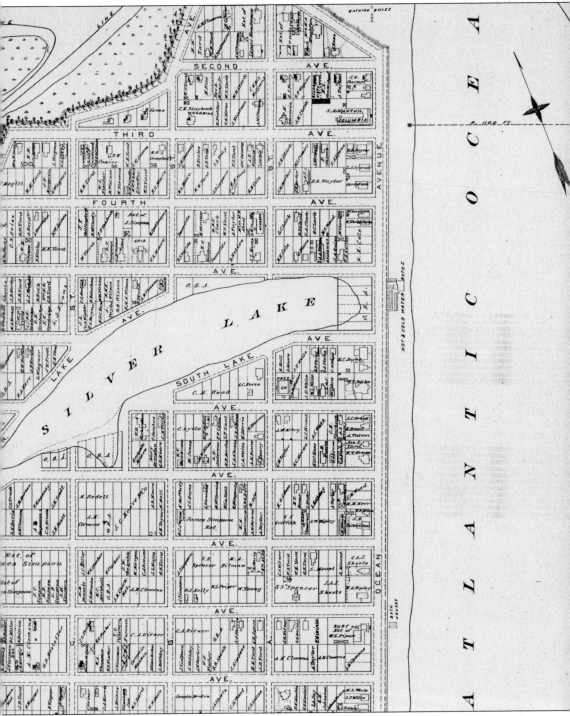

The estate of Isaac Henderson is marked between First and Second Avenues. The original Buena Vista Hotel is on Second Avenue and the Columbia Hotel is on the corner of Third and Ocean Avenues. (Moss Archives.)

Opened in 1878, the Columbia House at Third and Ocean Avenues attracted a well-to-do crowd and boasted a barbershop, billiard hall, bowling alley, telegraph office, call bells, and gas and water throughout. The way this engraving shows absolutely nothing else in the background is noteworthy, but whether or not this artist's depiction was accurate is debatable.

The Neptune House, according to the 1878 *Woolman and Rose Historical and Biographical Atlas of the New Jersey Coast*, "commands an unobstructed view of the ocean for many miles up and down the beach, giving to the lover of nature, from its piazza, one of nature's grandest pictures, and to the invalid, the invigorating benefit of its air." (Virginia Slusser.)

An engraving of the Kansas and Colorado House as it appeared at the 1876 Philadelphia Centennial Exposition provides evidence that the building underwent only moderate structural changes after it was moved to Ocean Beach and converted to a hotel. (Collection of T.J. McMahon, Fair Haven.)

The Colorado House, built from the old Kansas and Colorado buildings of the 1876 Philadelphia Centennial Exposition, occupied the entire block between Fourteenth and Fifteenth Avenues on the oceanfront and had over one hundred rooms. It is said that the "Sandy Hook lights" (probably a reference to the Twin Lights at Highlands) were visible from the hotel's tower. (Virginia Slusser.)

The Fifth Avenue House, located on the banks of the Shark River, "commands a magnificent view of the ocean and river," as described in the 1878 *Woolman and Rose Historical and Biographical Atlas of the New Jersey Coast*. The proprietor, Mr. J.L. Hoppock, also built the Neptune House by the sea and had a good reputation for his "untiring devotion in affording amusement for the young people." (Virginia Slusser.)

An 1879 advertisement for an Ocean Beach real estate auction aims to lure prospective buyers to the area with a clambake, collation, and music. (Virginia Slusser.)

An 1882 photograph of Buhler's Pavilion on the Shark River, where boats could be rented and bait purchased (now the site of the Belmar Marina), shows railroad tracks in front of the boathouse. (Laurie McEvoy.)

Silhouetted in front of Buhler's boat rental house on the Shark River, "Ida and Mrs. Thompson" and an unidentified man are enjoying a peaceful day by the river c. 1880s at Ocean Beach. (Laurie McEvoy.)

This Seaside Ice wagon probably dates from the 1880s. The "SS" Ice Company appears on the 1889 *Wolverton Atlas of Monmouth County*'s map of Ocean Beach on the corner of Ninth Avenue and E Street. (Laurie McEvoy.)

This image of the store and residence of D.A.Walling at Ocean Beach from the 1878 *Woolman and Rose Historical and Biographical Atlas of the New Jersey Coast* may be one of the earliest depictions of a Belmar shopping district.

Two

Hotels by the Sea
After 1889

A Belmar landmark for many years, the Columbia Hotel on the corner of Third and Ocean Avenues was originally the Columbia House, built in 1878 (see p. 16). In 1893, the hotel was rebuilt after a storm; it was remodeled again in 1917. This postcard view is c. 1905.

The Delaware Building at the 1876 Philadelphia Centennial Exposition is depicted here as it looked at the fair before being moved to Ocean Beach. A wrap-around porch was added when it became an oceanfront hotel. At least six buildings from the centennial ended up in Ocean Beach, and possibly more. (Collection of T.J. McMahon, Fair Haven.)

The Delaware House on the northwest corner of Thirteenth and Ocean Avenues, shown here as it appeared in about 1910, was originally the old Delaware State Building from the Philadelphia Centennial Exposition. (Belmar Public Library.)

The Marlborough Hotel is still recognizable as the former Delaware House after some remodeling, c. 1920. The Delaware coat of arms continued to be displayed above the front porch. (Belmar Public Library.)

The Neptune Hotel at Sixteenth and Ocean Avenues was The Neptune House as depicted on p. 16 when Belmar was known as Ocean Beach. This postcard shows the hotel as it looked c. 1910. (Belmar Public Library.)

The Colorado Hotel at Fourteenth and Ocean Avenues looked much the same in about 1910 as it did when it was the Colorado House, a building moved from the 1876 Philadelphia Centennial Exposition in the days when Belmar was Ocean Beach, as seen on p. 17. (Belmar Public Library.)

The aftermath of the fire that totally destroyed the Colorado Hotel in 1922 is captured in this dramatic photograph. (Belmar Historical Council.)

The Buena Vista Hotel on Second Avenue was a fashionable big hotel. The original Buena Vista at the same location dates back to the days when Belmar was Ocean Beach, as seen on p. 10. This postcard view is *c.* 1920.

The Carleton Hotel, as depicted here *c.* 1920, was on the corner of Ninth and Ocean Avenues. Although the Carleton is thought to have been converted from an 1876 Philadelphia Centennial Exposition building, there is no proof at this time. (Belmar Public Library.)

The huge Machinery Hall at the 1876 Philadelphia Centennial Exposition was broken up into smaller sections and redesigned as other structures. Sections of Machinery Hall became the Atlantic Hotel that occupied the oceanfront block between Fifteenth and Sixteenth Avenues. The postcard above of the Atlantic is *c.* 1905.

The Atlantic Hotel was drastically redesigned, and some sections were joined together as depicted on this card that was postmarked in 1918.

In 1922, a group of bathers are enjoying the beach at Sixteenth Avenue in front of the Atlantic Hotel. The person in the center of the photograph is wearing a long black robe, an intriguing bathing costume to say the least. (Collection of John Walsifer.)

By 1927, the Atlantic Hotel had undergone another major facelift and now the familiar brick entrance with three arches is seen, as well as the obvious addition of a tennis court.

The McCann's Atlantic Hotel, formerly the Atlantic Hotel, is seen here as it appeared around 1939 or 1940. During World War II, Patrick McCann, a hard-working Irish immigrant who was living in Newark, decided to rent the downstairs bar at the Atlantic Hotel in Belmar. Times were tough during the Great Depression and the war years. McCann wanted to leave the city to make a better life for his wife Kathleen and their three children. The bar business was booming because of the influx of soldiers and sailors into Fort Monmouth and the Earle Navy Depot, both near Belmar. However, the hotel room bookings were not so good. People were hesitant to stay on the New Jersey Shore because oil washed up on the beaches from tankers that were being torpedoed off the coast by German submarines. Patrick McCann soon purchased the hotel and the entire family went to work. Pat ran the bar while his wife managed the hotel and the kids even doubled as bellhops. According to Pat McCann Jr., "As the tide of the war turned in favor of the Allies, the beach got better and the hotel business took off." The bar was leased out to Vince McCarthy, redecorated with a tropical theme, and called the "Aloha" in the late 1940s. McCann took over the bar again in the mid-fifties, and it became the "Claddagh Inn." In the early 1960s, McCann sold the hotel. In 1972, the historic building burned to the ground. (Pat McCann Jr.)

The McCann family and a group of summer visitors assemble for a portrait in front of the McCann's Atlantic Hotel between Fifteenth and Sixteenth Avenues in the 1940s. (Pat McCann Jr.)

In about 1939 or 1940, proprietor Pat McCann Sr. stands ready and waiting for summer patrons at McCann's Bar and Grill at McCann's Atlantic Hotel. Don't miss the two delightful coconuts with painted faces hanging above the bar, popular tropical souvenirs of the 1940s. (Pat McCann Jr.)

The Cochran House, as it was called in this turn-of-the-century view, still stands on Second Avenue near Ocean Avenue and is known as The White House.

The Cedars, a charming guesthouse on Second Avenue, pictured here in about 1910, was originally the Woodbine Cottage when Belmar was known as Ocean Beach. (Moss Archives.)

Three
The Beach and Boardwalk

Gordon's Pavilion is seen from the beach in this c. 1910 photograph. Parasols were in favor to protect the women's delicate complexions from the sun. However, the gentleman to the right seems to be in need of shade as much as the lady on the left. (Belmar Public Library.)

Gordon's Pavilion, Belmar, N. J.

1910

The Fifth Avenue Pavilion leased by James Gordon in 1881 was opened in 1894 under the name of William F. Gordon and was known as Gordon's Pavilion. In this c. 1910 postcard, some young people are casually sitting outside looking at the cameraman who is apparently standing in the middle of Ocean Avenue. (Belmar Public Library.)

A 1906 view of Gordon's Pavilion features two men with an interesting-looking cart, perhaps a rolling chair to take a tourist for a ride? (Collection of John Walsifer.)

A group of spectators gazes intently upon a diver in action at Gordon's Swimming Pool, located at Gordon's Fifth Avenue pavilion *c*. 1915. This image appears in a reverse format on the cover of this book. (Belmar Public Library.)

At Gordon's Swimming Pool, a crowd watches a swim meet *c*. 1915. (Belmar Public Library.)

This lineup of young women on an excursion to Belmar in August 1908 resembles an early version of the Radio City Music Hall Rockettes. The caption handwritten on the photograph says "More than 16 to 1," referring, of course, to the one man who seems to be keeping a watchful eye on the women. (Collection of John Walsifer.)

In this photo card, the same group of young women as seen above is fishing from the pier at Belmar. The handwriting says, "Call of the Wild." The lone man continues to chaperone the group. (Collection of John Walsifer.)

A real photo postcard view from the early 1900s provides a good look at the boardwalk that appears level with the street. The scene is near Eleventh Avenue. (Collection of John Walsifer.)

A woman with a baby carriage waits to cross Ocean Avenue at Tenth Street in this *c.* 1912 postcard. (Belmar Public Library.)

The woman wearing the long dress in the center of this image appears to be holding a small box camera and preparing to take a photograph of her friends in their bathing costumes on the Belmar beach on July 25, 1915. (Belmar Public Library.)

Bathers on the Belmar beach on July 31, 1915, are wearing the typical unrevealing bathing costumes of the era, but styles would soon begin to change after World War I. (Belmar Public Library.)

Kathleen and Pat McCann Sr. are enjoying the sunny Belmar beach in the early 1920s, although some people have apparently chosen to go under the boardwalk for shade. The identity of the man on the left is unknown. (Pat McCann Jr.)

This artistic-looking photograph shows a view of Belmar from under the Eighth Avenue jetty after a storm on November 10, 1932. The Belmar Fishing Club and pier can be seen in the distance. (Birdsall Engineering, Inc.)

Fashionable Japanese-style parasols keep the sun off these four Belmar bathing beauties in the early 1920s. On the far left is Mildred Henning (Mildred Desmond Day of Belmar), who located this photograph among her souvenirs.

This view shows a cluster of bathers at the Second Avenue beach. The old Belmar Fishing Club is in the rear of the photograph and the Columbia Hotel is on the right. (Belmar Public Library.)

Jaunty automobiles cruise up and down Ocean Avenue, probably looking for parking spaces, on August 23, 1925. This view looking south includes the Fifth Avenue Pavilion and illustrates how it rested on high pilings. The beach eventually became even with the tops of the pilings. (Moss Archives.)

Another photograph of Ocean Avenue taken on the same date as the photograph above shows the view to the north with the old Belmar Fishing Club and pier in the background. Observe how the parking spaces are filled up. Apparently, parking meters were not used in those days. (Moss Archives.)

Belmar, N.J., Sanborn's Pavilion.

Sanborn's Pavilion opened in 1903. It replaced the old Tenth Avenue Bath Houses built in 1879. On this c. 1912 postcard view, it is interesting to see how the women sit directly on the sand, long skirts and all. (Belmar Public Library Collection.)

By the early 1930s, Sanborn's Pavilion had undergone a few structural changes and had become simply the Tenth Avenue Pavilion. Notice the difference in the length of the pilings that are longer in this postcard view than the earlier one.

The New Tenth Avenue Pavilion, built in the 1940s and owned by the borough, burned down in a disastrous fire on Labor Day, 1963. (Belmar Public Library.)

"Beach scene showing new pavilion" is the caption on the back of this postcard. This is the modern pavilion that replaced the "New" Tenth Avenue Pavilion after the 1963 fire.

Inside the restaurant at the Tenth Pavilion about 1952, Barney Granoff, known to everyone as "Pop," cuts the cake for his 62nd birthday. On his right is his nephew, Melvyn Krauss, and seated between two unidentified girls is his granddaughter, Sandra Granoff. Standing fifth from the left is his son, Irving Granoff, and seated at the table on the right are his granddaughter, Ronnie Granoff, and Irving's wife, Teddy. Others are unidentified. (Sandra Epstein.)

From left to right are Irving Granoff, his nephew Melvyn Krauss, and Irving's brother Seymour (a professional photographer). This picture was taken outside the Tenth Avenue Pavilion in the 1940s. (Sandra Epstein.)

Howard Rowland (left) and Barney "Pop" Granoff smile for the camera on the Belmar boardwalk in about 1952. (Sandra Epstein.)

Howard Rowland, the handsome and famous head of the Belmar lifeguards for whom the Tenth Avenue Pavilion is named today, poses here with his dog, Ming. The photograph was taken at John's Blue Lunch at Nineteenth Street and Ocean Avenue in the early 1950s. (Robert V. Pringle.)

Belmar lifeguards pose for their annual group portrait in 1945. From left to right are (front row) unknown, Jeannie Bunk, Jack Ivins, unknown, Police Sergeant Bill Briden, Howard Rowland, Jimmy Raymond, Bob Pringle, Ray Darby, and Herb Scuorzo; (back row) Al Zimijursk, Emil Gennell, Art Bauer, Bill Wilson, Bill Barry, Dick Seifert, Ken Roberts, John Stanley, Brandt Clark, and unknown. (Robert V. Pringle.)

The Belmar lifeguards of 1947 are as follows: (front row) D. Distasio, Otto Reinach, Ed Laux, and Herb Scuorzo; (second row) Sergeant Bill Briden, Dick Siefert, unknown, Bill Wilson, unknown, and Howard Rowland; (third row) unknown, Bob Croste, Bill Kennedy, Jerry Britton, ? Cannon, and unknown; (back row) unknown, Dick Meyler, unknown, Art Bauer, Bob Pringle, Bob McEntee, and Bob "Red" Williams. (Robert V. Pringle.)

In August 1932, crowds jam the beach and boardwalk in this photograph taken from the Tenth Avenue Pavilion. The beach was created by the Eighth Avenue jetty that can be seen in the distance. (Moss Archives.)

This aerial view taken in the 1930s defines the Belmar beach, boardwalk, and pavilions looking north. The gates leading to Spring Lake are in the foreground. (Moss Archives.)

A 1930s aerial shot of the Shark River Inlet looking south gives a view of the Shark River Inlet Bridge and the Belmar Fishing Club in the upper right. In the lower half of the photograph that shows the north side of the bridge, there is a vacant area of Avon-by-the-Sea that is now developed. (Moss Archives.)

This magnificent 1930s view from the air, looking south, reveals the Shark River Inlet Bridge with the gates up. The large building on Ocean Avenue is the Columbia Hotel and just to its right on Second Avenue is the Buena Vista Hotel, both gone now. The easily recognizable Belmar Fishing Club that still stands today is on the left. (Birdsall Engineering, Inc.)

The Belmar Fishing Club at First and Ocean Avenues was founded in 1909. Situated on land that once belonged to the Ocean Beach Association, the original clubhouse is depicted here with a billboard announcing that a new clubhouse is to be erected. (Belmar Fishing Club.)

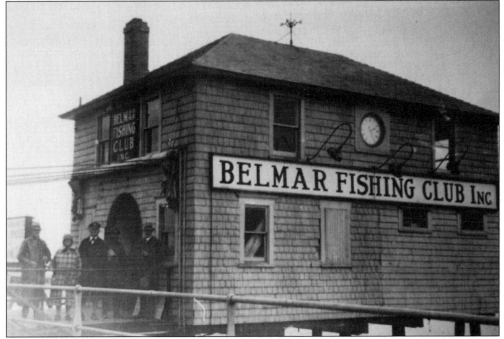

On September 1, 1909, the Belmar Fishing Club was organized with forty-nine charter members. This view of the original clubhouse reveals a clock on the south side of the building. (Belmar Fishing Club.)

The old Belmar Fishing Club building and the pier as they looked in the early years of the century are frequently visible in the backgrounds of beach photographs from the early 1900s.

In 1912, a group of Belmar Fishing Club members show off the weakfish they caught. From left to right are Geo Bloomsburg, Al Ackerman, Ed Pinnett, John Watson, Charlie Meehan, Jesse Meekers, Ed Suret, Bill Dear, Harry Douty, Frank Reynolds, Henry Herberman, and Herberman's chauffeur. Don't you wonder if these men wore the suits and ties while fishing? (Belmar Fishing Club.)

The "mission-style" Belmar Fishing Club of today appears much the same as it did when it was dedicated on May 30, 1930. Continued growth of the club warranted the new building for the members of the private social and sporting institution. In 1940, the pier was extended, but the new section and much of the old pier were destroyed in the Hurricane of 1944. A new pier was dedicated in July 1946.

The Belmar Fishing Club took a beating from the Hurricane of 1944 that ripped apart much of the New Jersey Shore. This photograph shows the damage to the entrance to the club after the storm. (Birdsall Engineering, Inc.)

Lounge Room Looking West

The interior of the Belmar Fishing Club's main lounge in 1939 looks much like the lobby of a classy hotel of the era. The stone fireplace and wood-beamed ceiling give it a warm and cozy atmosphere. The border of fish on the tops of the walls is, of course, an appropriate decoration.

Assembly Room Looking West

The upstairs assembly room of the Belmar Fishing Club appears bright and cheery in this depiction from a 1939 brochure. There are spectacular views of the shoreline from either side of this room, facing north or south.

Fishermen are enjoying a day at the old Belmar Fishing Club pier in the 1930s. The club's motto is "For the Glory of the Sport." A 1939 brochure describes the club as "the largest and most progressive and influential surf-angling and sports Club on the Atlantic seaboard." (Belmar Fishing Club.)

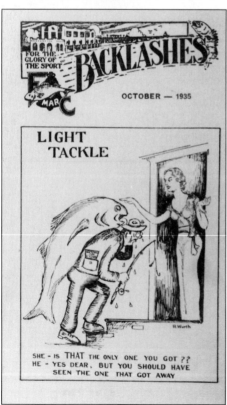

Each month, *Backlashes*, the Belmar Fishing Club's newsletter, would feature an amusing cartoon on the cover such as this one from October 1935. (Belmar Fishing Club.)

A crowd stands on the pier of the Belmar Fishing Club for the dedication of an extension to the pier on what must have been an unusually chilly May 30, 1940, judging from the clothing worn. In the background, the Buena Vista Hotel that was on Second Avenue is on the left. (Belmar Fishing Club.)

In this recent photograph, Tom Gallagher, past president, and Fred Sigrist, current president of the Belmar Fishing Club, flank a c. 1930 portrait of President Herbert Hoover, who autographed his likeness for the club. The Tap Room of the clubhouse contains memorabilia including photographs of Benjamin Farrier, the club's well-respected president for many years, and of celebrities who visited.

Augustus "Gus" Wooley (1861–1933) operated the Wall Fishery at Belmar in the early 1900s. In the late 1800s, Gus worked for E. Walter Bennett at the Iron's Fish Pound at Seventeenth and Ocean Avenues in Belmar, and changed the name when he purchased the business. Gus Wooley's great-grandson, Dick Napoliton of Wall Township, provided this portrait from the turn of the century.

Wooley's fishing boats are seen here in July 1912. Workhorses were employed to pull the boats in and out of the water. (Dick Napoliton.)

A rare postcard of pound fishermen at Belmar from the early 1900s does not give any details as to the location of the fishing shanty that appears to be resting on cinderblocks. (Dick Napoliton.)

Although the image on this postcard from 1907 of a boy on a shark might be a generic photo card not representing a Belmar scene, it was mailed as a Belmar souvenir and is simply too cute to leave out of this volume.

In this photograph from April 25, 1925, men are repairing damage on Eighteenth Avenue resulting from a storm. Note that although automobiles were prevalent, horses still did much of the work in the 1920s. (Birdsall Engineering, Inc.)

Belmar Mayor VanNote is viewing a washout at Nineteenth Avenue that occurred due to a storm in April 1926. (Belmar Historical Council.)

On a hot summer day in 1932, some bathers have decided to enjoy the shade of the boardwalk. The Eighth Avenue jetty is seen in the back of this photograph. (Birdsall Engineering, Inc.)

The 1929 Thirteenth Avenue Pavilion that has housed a McDonald's restaurant since 1983 is seen here from a distance on August 11, 1932. There are very few examples of pavilions like this left at the New Jersey Shore. (Birdsall Engineering, Inc.)

People are out after the Hurricane of 1944 to look at the damage done to the Belmar boardwalk. (Birdsall Engineering, Inc.)

This roof at an unidentified Belmar beach location was totally ripped off a house due to the high winds from the Hurricane of 1944. (Birdsall Engineering, Inc.)

The devastating damage to the Belmar boardwalk from the Hurricane of 1944 is evident in this photograph, which looks towards the Tenth Avenue Pavilion. (Birdsall Engineering, Inc.)

Although surrounded by damage from the Hurricane of 1944, the sturdy Thirteenth Avenue Pavilion looks to be in great shape. The 1929 building that was converted to a McDonald's restaurant in 1983 continues to survive today. (Birdsall Engineering, Inc.)

The Hurricane of 1944 that cost New Jersey $25 million in damages ripped out an entire chunk of the Sixteenth Avenue Fishing Pier. (Birdsall Engineering, Inc.)

This photograph provides a closer look at the damage to the Sixteenth Avenue Fishing Pier. (Birdsall Engineering, Inc.)

A dramatic view of an airship flying over the ocean near Gordon's Pavilion was taken in July 1918. The Belmar Fishing Club and pier are visible in the background. (Belmar Public Library.)

"Dorr's monoplane" appears to be protected with covers. There was an airstrip on the inlet terrace area before homes were built. This photograph is from 1913. (Belmar Public Library.)

The writing on this photograph reads, "Hydroplane wrecked at Belmar, August the 1st, 1919, photo by L.A. Waldron, Belmar, N.J." This crash scene was near Carpenter's Pavilion (at the Shark River, now the marina). (Collection of John Walsifer.)

A real photograph of an airplane with the Belmar Fishing Club and pier in the background was pasted onto this commemorative envelope of a special air service flight on May 19, 1938. (Richard Neral.)

Four

In Honor of
the Rescuers

In their first "three engine photo," members of the Union Fire Co. No. 1 show off their equipment c. 1910. From left to right are William Robinson Sr., Clarence Stines, Lucius Davenport, Jesse Shibal, George Heyniger, William Rovingson Jr., Valentine Hausotte, Dr. Stanley Palmateer, Henry Cooper, and George Titus. (Union Fire Co. No. 1.)

The Union Fire Co. No. 1 purchased its "Button" pumper in 1892. It is covered with children in this first company photograph. (Union Fire Co. No. 1.)

Belmar firemen pose with "Uncle Sam," who is apparently on stilts behind them, and their trusty beagle. The photograph dates to the early years of the century. (Goodwill Hose Co. No. 1.)

The Belmar Fire Department is pictured in front of the Columbia Hotel before the organization of the Goodwill Hose Co. No. 1 in 1901. The Union company's first hose wagon, built by the members, is seen in this photograph. (R. Conklin.)

In October 1939, a raging fire destroyed the landmark Columbia Hotel. Pictured is all that remained of the elegant old hotel after the blaze. (Union Fire Co. No. 1.)

Belmar's Volunteer Hook and Ladder Company, founded in 1894, is shown in front of the Belmar Public School in the early 1900s. The photograph appeared in the *New York Sunday World* newspaper. (Garry Young.)

Looking spiffy in their summer whites, members of the Union Fire Co. No. 1 prepare to march in a 1922 Red Bank parade. From left to right are as follows: (front row) unknown, unknown, George Heyniger, unknown, Bill Robinson, William Cooper, A. Davenport, unknown,and L. Davenport; (back row) Val Hausotte, William Robinson Sr., and Dessa Shibla. (Union Fire Co. No. 1.)

The Volunteer Hook and Ladder Company parades down F Street during the 1914 celebration for the laying of the library cornerstone. (Belmar Public Library.)

The Union Fire Co. No. 1 wagon with Estelle, Sonnenberg, and Davenport aboard, followed by The Goodwill Hose Co. No. 1 "Pinfeathers" rig, were pulled by their dependable horses at the 1914 parade. The horses were well known and well loved by the fire companies. (Belmar Public Library.)

In this photograph from the early 1900s, loaned by the Goodwill Hose Co. No. 1 are from left to right: Jerry Lehman (driver), Bill Awlpack, Dick Wines, Clinton Cooper, Rod Danson, Arthur Havsole, and Henry Reimelleron (on the step).

In 1952, Larry Vola, Fire Chief (later to be Police Chief), congratulates Herman Hausotte, a charter member of the Goodwill Hose Co. No. 1, on fifty years in the company. (Goodwill Hose Co. No. 1.)

The Goodwill Hose Co. No. 1's 1869 "Button" steam-powered pumper was first used by the Union Fire Co. No. 1 before being given to Goodwill in the company's early years. This historic pumper and the original Button pumper at the Union Fire Co. No. 1 are both well maintained, displayed at the respective firehouses and at special events. (Goodwill Hose Co. No. 1.)

The busy firemen repairing the wheel of Goodwill's "Button" pumper c. 1950s are, from left to right in front by the wheel, unknown, Tim Whitley, Don Heyniger, E. Cavanaugh Sr., and Cy Heyniger. In the back center is Connie Frosch. (Goodwill Hose Co. No. 1.)

Members of the Goodwill Hose Co. No. 1 proudly showed off their 1946 Seagrave Engine when it was new. From left to right are F. Vogt, unknown, Ennis Pierce, R. Riggs, and John Taylor. (Goodwill Hose Co. No. 1.)

In a modern photograph, the Union Fire Co. No. 1's 1968 Hahn, 1982 Prisch, and 1956 Seagrave are parked in front of the Union firehouse building on Ninth Avenue and E Street that was built in 1910. It housed the borough hall until 1920, the police department until 1984, and still houses the Union Fire Co. today. (Photograph by Ed Vetrecin.)

Trick or Treat? No, this group is ready to entertain the children at the Belmar Fire Department's annual children's Christmas party in 1946. Standing in front of the Rivoli Theater on F Street are, from left to right, Joe Gillen, Spence Clawson, an unknown bear, Russ Allgor as Santa Claus, Police Chief Joseph Isola as himself, Frank Vogt, and Howard Hoagland. (Union Fire Co. No. 1.)

A large group of happy children assembles in front of the Rivoli Theater on F Street in the 1940s for the annual Belmar Fire Department Christmas party photograph. (Collection of Dennis Lewis.)

In 1927, young Frank Mihlon Jr. stands proudly with his father, Frank Mihlon, the benefactor responsible for the first ambulance, uniforms, and property belonging to the Belmar First Aid Squad on Ninth Avenue. Because so many people were coming to the New Jersey Shore in the 1920s with the increased use of the automobile, it became apparent that an organized first aid squad was needed. According to Frank Jr., it all began when an angry man was locked out of his car in 1926. The car was parked on Ocean Avenue near the Mihlon house. The impatient man punched his fist through the car window. There was no safety glass in those days, and he cut an artery and some tendons. Fortunately, a doctor who was a summer visitor at the Columbia Hotel nearby saved the man. Seeing that man hurt from the accident made a big impression on young Frank, who can never forget that terrible sight. When Frank returned to the Belmar Public School at the end of that summer, he told custodian Charlie Berger about the incident. Berger explained that Belmar resident Charlie Measure had recently started a first aid squad that was then part of the fire department. Measure, who was a corpsman in World War I, had experience with war casualties. Frank Mihlon Jr. says Measure was "the perfect person to establish a civilian first aid squad." Young Mihlon began a crusade to help, and his father, Frank Mihlon Sr., a professional sports promoter known as "the Bicycle Czar of America," provided the things that were needed. And that was the beginning of the Belmar First Aid Squad that has the distinction of being known as the country's first first aid squad. (Frank Mihlon Jr.)

In a 1972 parade in Belmar, Frank Mihlon Jr. rides a float commemorating the pioneer first aid squad that was possible thanks to the generosity of his father. The boy portraying Frank as a child is wearing Frank's original first aid uniform. (Frank Mihlon Jr.)

Frank Mihlon Jr. is pictured in this charming portrait as a child in the 1920s with his mother, Minnie Yetter, a beautiful actress who appeared in many silent films. (Frank Mihlon Jr.)

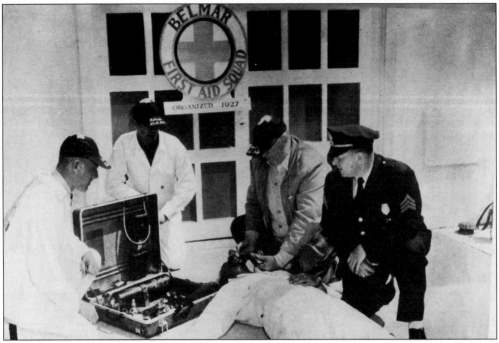

"First Aid Squad of Belmar, the pioneer organization in action" was the description given to this photograph in the *Newark Sunday News* on July 6, 1952. From left to right are John A. Kolb, Spencer Clawson, Charles Measure (organizer and first president), and Sergeant William Bridon. Ernest Davenport is the "victim." (Richard Neral.)

This building complex in a park-like setting is the home of the Belmar First Aid Squad on Ninth Avenue. The corner window shaped like a cross is an interesting feature. A plaque by the garage on the right pays tribute to Dr. Daniel C. Traverso (1899–1936), a local physician who helped the first aid squad and was greatly appreciated by the community.

Five
Along the Shark River

An artist's depiction on a postcard from the early 1900s illustrates Buhler's Pavilion at Tenth Avenue on the Shark River (now the area of the Belmar Marina) with a picnic grove, boats for hire, and swings for the children.

Buhler's Pavilion is shown here as it looked around 1905. In the building there was a bait and tackle shop. (Belmar Public Library.)

Sometime later, this front section was added on to Buhler's Pavilion when it was owned by W.H. Carpenter and then called Carpenter's Pavilion. An ice cream parlor was added as seen here, with a sign advertising ice cream sodas. (Belmar Public Library.)

Out on the pier at Buhler's Pavilion *c.* 1910, a sign reads, "Take a trip around the river in the launch River Queen or Annie B, Fare 25 cents."

Tents provided inexpensive lodging for summer visitors at the New Jersey Shore. This *c.* 1910 view is of the tent camp at Buhler's Grove along the Shark River. (Belmar Public Library.)

In this *c.* 1912 postcard of the River Road, Buhler's Grove and Pavilion can be seen on the right and the Riverside House is down the road. (Belmar Public Library.)

The Riverside House, with a magnificent view from most every window, represents an elegant hotel of the early twentieth century. It was owned by Edward F. Lang. (Belmar Public Library.)

A 1907 postcard of the Shark River from Buhler's boat landing provides a tranquil scene with mirror-like reflections. The old Belmar Yacht Club is in the background, and Bennett's boathouse can be seen behind the yacht club. The triangular piece of land in this northwestern part of Belmar along the Shark River in the area of Pine Tree Way and Maplewood Avenue is known as Rhode Island Point.

A sporty automobile is parked in front of the old Belmar Yacht Club on River and Eleventh Avenues c. 1920. A new yacht club replaced it in 1928 at Oakwood and River Avenues, but no longer exists today.

This rare photograph is of Bennett's boathouse on the Shark River. The old yacht club is next door. (R. Conklin.)

Chute the Chutes, a fun and adventurous ride in its day, was located in the area of Fifth Avenue and F Street before Murphy's Casino was built. (Goodwill Hose Co. No. 1.)

A 1905 view of the Old F Street Bridge shows the boathouse owned by A.H. Riggs that was situated right in the middle of the bridge. (Collection of John Walsifer.)

This postcard provides a closer look at the boathouse in the middle of the Old F Street Bridge that is seen from a distance in the view above. (Collection of John Walsifer.)

The trolley tracks ran right in front of Murphy's Casino at Fifth Avenue and F Street by the Old F Street Bridge as depicted here c. 1920. (Belmar Public Library.)

This postcard from 1921 of the Old F Street Bridge over the Shark River gives a good idea of the activity on the busy bridge, including automobile and pedestrian traffic. (Collection of John Walsifer.)

"Clang, clang, clang went the trolley, ding, ding, ding went the bell . . ." The Atlantic Coast Electric Railway Company trolley that ran between Belmar and Asbury Park is headed north. Murphy's Casino is seen right in back of it. (Collection of Harold Solomon.)

A 1929 advertisement for Murphy's Casino describes menu selections. A $3 shore dinner, billed as "the best on earth," was available, as well as simply a special dinner for half that price.

BELMAR CASINO

(THOMAS MURPHY, Prop.)

Special Shore Dinner $3.00

Olives	Pickles	Radishes

Clam Chowder

Steamed Soft Clams	Cup of Clam Broth

Filet of Sole, Saute Meuniere

Broiled Live Lobster	Soft Shell Crab

Potatoes	Corn

Chicken

Cheese and Crackers	Bread and Butter

Home Made Mince Pie or Chilled Watermellon

Tea	Coffee	Milk

THE BEST ON EARTH

Our Special Dinner $1.50

RESTAURANT A LA CARTE

ACCOMMODATION FOR 1,000

SPACIOUS BALL ROOM	BOAT DOCK

SHARK RIVER & F ST.

BELMAR, NEW JERSEY

A solitary horse and buggy crosses the Shark River Bridge (the Old F Street Bridge) in this popular postcard, created *c.* 1905. (Collection of John Walsifer.)

A launch cruises gently along the Shark River, perhaps going to pick up waiting tourists at Buhler's Pavilion's dock. (R. Conklin.)

A 1929 postcard shows the "Shark River Inlet and New [Route 35] Bridge." The question is, did the bathing beauty seen in the lower right of the photograph really dive into the swift current of the river? Tune in next week to find out! (John Walsifer Collection.)

John W. Kidd's boathouse and recreational area (called the Fort Comfort Pavilion) at the south end of the Old F Street Bridge was known by many visitors simply as Captain Kidd's. (Dennis Lewis Collection.)

"A Picturesque Road Along Shark River, Belmar, N.J." is the title on this 1910 postcard. The dirt road and trees give the area a rustic look, but the telephone poles give evidence that civilization is close by.

A section of an aerial view of the Belmar Marina when it was under construction in the mid-1930s shows many changes along Route 35. The photograph is cut off on the top at F Street. (Belmar Historical Council.)

This photograph is of the Belmar Marine Basin as it looked in 1942. (Goodwill Hose Co. No. 1.)

A crowd is "Watching the boats at dock after a day's catch" at the Belmar Marina according to the caption on this 1950s postcard. (Collection of John Walsifer.)

This is an unusual photograph of an early dredge on the Shark River in 1913. (Belmar Public Library.)

WHERE SHARK RIVER MEETS THE ATLANTIC OCEAN
AT BELMAR. N. J.

circa 1920

"Where the Shark River Meets the Atlantic Ocean at Belmar NJ" is the caption on this c. 1920 postcard. It is surprising that postcards were made to depict topics such as construction. One usually thinks of postcards as featuring more scenic views, but maintaining the inlet has always been of great interest and importance. (Belmar Public Library.)

Party boats loaded with fishermen are a familiar sight at Belmar's marina. The well-known *Miss Belmar* is shown here in the 1950s. The boat is said to have been a former PT boat that was converted for recreational use and painted pink. (Collection of John Walsifer.)

The Shark River Inlet Bridge, built in 1937 between Belmar and Avon-by-the-Sea, is open in this *c.* 1960s photograph, allowing a party boat, the *Optimist Queen*, to return to the Belmar Marina.

The lowlands along the Shark River from the ocean to F street that were purchased by Paul T. Zizinia in 1915 were filled in and an upscale residential development known as Inlet Terrace was constructed. The 1917 postcard above is of the Inlet Terrace Club, a social club for the residents that has now been converted to a private home. (Belmar Public Library.)

A 1944 aerial view gives a clear picture of the area known as Inlet Terrace, built upon low land that was filled in. (Robert L. White.)

Six

Main Street and Around Town

Always a hub of activity, Belmar's F Street is also known simply as Main Street. This postcard view, c. 1905, shows the corner of Ninth Avenue and Main Street looking north. The building on the left with the tower is the site of today's Don's Pizza King, next to Pyanoe Plaza. The trolley can be seen in the background.

Belmar had several pharmacies in the early twentieth century. The Seaside Pharmacy at 701 F
Street, owned by R.S. Wines, had a soda fountain as most of the pharmacies did in the old days.
This photo postcard reveals an interior of the Seaside Pharmacy c. 1905, with neat and tidy
rows of medicine jars. (Collection of Shirley Carroll.)

Pharmacist Robert Kasdan, known as Doc, delivered his special "Digestive Mixture" in this
truck. His formula included belladonna, essence of pepsin, rhubarb, and soda, among other
things. Enthusiastic customers said it relieved their gastric distress. Kasdan even received letters
from Belmar summer visitors who wanted to order it all winter. (Claire Angrist.)

The Kasdan family poses for a portrait about 1905. From left to right are Robert (pharmacist), his daughter Sylvia, his father Jacob (a founder of the Sons of Israel Congregation on Eleventh Avenue), his wife Mary, his son Ben, his mother Fannie, his sister Rose, and his son Alfred. Daughter Claire Kasdan Angrist of Belmar, who provided this photograph, explains that she and her twin brother, Clarence, are not in this photograph because they were born later, in 1909.

The Kasdan Pharmacy on the northwest corner of Tenth and F Streets, depicted here in about 1910, was on the site of what is now the McGowan Agency. Kasdan opened a new store at Fifteenth and F Streets in 1916 that he operated until his retirement in 1938. When Claire Kasdan (now Angrist) was a toddler, she gave her parents quite a scare by walking on the railing of the balcony! (Belmar Public Library.)

The original Taylor & Johnson furniture and hardware store was on the east side of F Street between Seventh and Eighth Avenues. Paul C. Taylor opened this store in 1894 with Joe Johnson of Point Pleasant. The Johnsons were well known for their hardware business in Point Pleasant. See chapter seven for more about the Taylor family. (Collection of John Walsifer.)

The Taylor store is seen here after it moved to the northeast corner of Ninth and F Streets. This is now the site of Thrift Drug, formerly Schatzow's Variety Store. (Collection of John Walsifer.)

On July 31, 1914, a parade commemorated the laying of the cornerstone for the new Belmar Public Library on Tenth Avenue. Lodge members, probably Masons, are seen marching south on F Street near Ninth Avenue. The Taylor & Johnson store can be seen across from the First National Bank. (Belmar Public Library.)

The Belmar First National Bank building on the southeast corner of Ninth and F Streets is now the Fleet Bank. In this photograph, it is covered with flags and banners during the 1914 festivities centering around the laying of the cornerstone for the library. (Belmar Public Library.)

Decorated for the parade to celebrate the laying of the library cornerstone in 1914, the Coast Gas Company makes an impressive appearance. (Belmar Public Library.)

Levinsohn's building at the southeast corner of Tenth Avenue and F Street is ready for the library cornerstone laying festivities in 1914. The building remains a local landmark today and houses several stores. (Belmar Public Library.)

In 1914, a group of children dressed in their Sunday best wait for the parade to begin. The old Chamberlain building can be seen behind them. (Belmar Public Library.)

This photograph was apparently taken at the library site on Tenth Avenue during the cornerstone-laying celebration. Perhaps the gentleman in the straw boater is looking between the two trees to see the ceremony? (Belmar Public Library.)

The Belmar Public Library began with a group of ladies who got together for tea in 1911 at the home of Louise Phillips. They opened the first library at 802 F Street in 1911 but the following year they moved it to 819 F Street for more space. The library continued to grow and the present library on Tenth Avenue, seen here in a postcard from 1928, opened in 1914. (Collection of Dennis Lewis.)

A recent photograph of the Belmar Public Library that was designed by architect Edward L. Tilton of New York and built by contractor Horace H. Moore of Spring Lake, shows that the exterior has not changed much except for the addition of a canopy and landscaping.

Lois Gallagher, who currently runs the Belmar Public Library, holds the original pastel artwork for a poster announcing the opening of the first Belmar library on Saturday, September 23, 1911. At that time there were about 407 books; by 1914 there were over 2,700 books. Today, the Carnegie-funded library has approximately 32,000 books and keeps up with the rapidly changing times and new forms of media.

On March 12, 1989, the Belmar Public Library's 75th anniversary entry won the trophy for best float at the annual Belmar St. Patrick's Day Parade. Riding on the float that says, "Belmar Library Celebrates The Year of the Young Reader," are Grace Roper, Mildred Day, Lois Gallagher, Lorraine Tosti, and Betty Ann Bower. This scene is somewhat reminiscent of the parade that was held in honor of the laying of the library cornerstone in 1914. (Lois Gallagher.)

circa 1905

Belmar, N.J., R.R. Depot.

When the railroad first came to Belmar, then Ocean Beach, in 1875, the influx of visitors began to increase. The old two-story depot is seen on this postcard *c.* 1905. This station was just north of the present one. (Belmar Public Library.)

9136

The new station, still in use today, is seen here *c.* 1920. Interestingly, the back side of the station by the parking lot has now been converted into a dentist's office. (Belmar Public Library.)

This great aerial view of Main or F Street dates from January 1947. The Belmar Public School is the large building in the upper right. The cross street in the bottom half with a Tydol gas station on the northeast corner is Eighth Avenue. (Collection of Dennis Lewis.)

A Depression-era version of today's fast food restaurant, Celia Brown's Belmar drive-in on the southwest corner of Eighteenth and F Streets (now Radio Station WRAT) featured car hops who hooked trays onto car windows. The big, juicy hamburgers cost 15¢. The Belmar staff posed with Celia's Asbury Park shop workers at the Belmar location for this 1937 portrait. (Raymond F. Davis.)

At H. Weinstein's New Refreshment Store, Sixteenth Avenue and F Street, patrons indulged in a variety of ice cream sodas made with Dolly Madison ice cream. (Collection of John Walsifer.)

A popular destination at the Jersey Shore for seafood was The Original Dave and Evelyn's run by Dave Sanderson and Evelyn Longstreet. They started out with a little stand to sell clams by the Old F Street Bridge during the Depression and the enterprise grew to be the landmark restaurant at 507 F Street (now Jack Baker's Lobster Shanty.). This 1950s postcard shows Evelyn's interior with knotty pine walls, sailfish, and oyster crackers on each table.

Dave and Evelyn later opened Dave's seafood restaurant at 700 F Street, but according to some local residents, this venture never received the acclaim that the original Evelyn's did and closed in the 1970s. The site with its familiar tower is Spike's Fish Market and Restaurant today.

The business district of Belmar in the 1950s will evoke memories for those who grew up in the borough as well as for summer visitors who shopped here while vacationing. Can you recognize some of those now classic cars in this postcard view? (Collection of Dennis Lewis.)

In about 1949, these five women are ready to roll in this snazzy automobile. From left to right, in the front are Ellen Krauss and Leonore Levine, and in the back seat are Anna Levine, Lena Rosenberg, and Ida Krauss. They are at Eleventh Avenue and B Street. (Sandra Epstein.)

Seven

Families, School, Worship, and Events

At their cozy bungalow on Twentieth Avenue in the early 1920s, Kathleen McCann is standing on the porch while her husband Pat holds little Marian. The identity of the man seated on the porch swing is not known. (Pat McCann Jr.)

The Taylor family lived in this house at 510 Sixth Avenue This photograph is from about 1905. (John A. Taylor.)

Paul C. Taylor, who ran the local hardware store (see p. 94), was mayor of Belmar for one year from 1905 to 1906. His son John A. Taylor worked in the family business and has been a very active member of the community over the years who is greatly admired. John A. Taylor, who provided this photograph of his father, became mayor some sixty-two years after his dad.

John A. Taylor, who would grow up to be mayor of Belmar from 1967 to 1979, is sitting on the chair with his brother Philip standing next to him in this adorable c. 1913 baby picture. Philip, a World War II veteran, later worked in sales for a business machine company. (John A. Taylor.)

Helen Pauline Taylor, the older sister of John A. and Philip, strikes a lovely and somewhat wistful pose in 1907. Born in 1900, she enjoyed art and created pottery. She worked at the Belmar Public School for some time and lived until 1988. (John A. Taylor.)

Former Mayor John A. Taylor recently identified most of his 1921 fourth-grade Belmar Public School classmates and could tell stories about many of them. The children he remembers in this class photograph are as follows: (front row) ? Glover, Meredith Heulitt, ? Wooley, Eugene Carpenter, John C. Taylor, unknown, Melvin Michaelson, unknown, unknown, David Weinstein, Ed Wisijohn, Karl Helbig, and Edison Reuben; (second row) Alice Lokerson, Pauline Hochberg, Alice Hurley, unknown, unknown, Harry Maltz, Sam Catalano, Archer Gibbons, unknown, and Roy Trasberg; (third row) Delsie Casagrande, Muriel Bearimore, Olga Heyniger, Edna Naylor, Celia Bunnin, Dorothy Haberstick, unknown, Harry Naylor, Charlie Farr, Gunner Guftafson, and unknown; (back row) unknown, William Lerner, and Miss Dorothy Pearce (the teacher, who later became Dorothy Daniels).

The Belmar Public School on F Street near Twelfth Avenue, said to be styled after Philadelphia's Independence Hall, is depicted on a 1910 postcard. It was also used as a high school but by 1912, the grammar school population had increased so greatly that it was necessary for Belmar students to use Asbury Park High School. (Collection of Dennis Lewis.)

A group of Belmar Public School faculty members assembled for this group photograph at a party given in E. Heyniger's's backyard in June 1953. (John A. Taylor.)

The 1936 Belmar Public School baseball team looks ready to take on any opponents. The man on the right is Thomas B. Harper, principal, who later became Monmouth County's superintendent of schools; on the left is the baseball coach, Lon Crandall. (Richard K. Sherman.)

The Belmar Public School Class of 1944 poses on the steps of the school (Robert V. Pringle.)

A group of Belmar women are gathered together for reasons unknown in the late forties or early fifties. They are, from left to right, (seated in the front row) Diane Harad, Ceil Grayer, Mildred Levy, and Kaye Makatansky; (standing in the back row) Shirley Steele, Reba Greenspan, Betty Weinstein, Madelyn Goldwyn, Ruth Biesky, and Babs Lasky. The photograph was taken by Steele's Photographic Service of Belmar. (Sandra Epstein.)

In this 1950s raffle, a state-of-the-art entertainment center was first prize, donated by the Jewish War Veterans of Belmar. From left to right are Belmar residents Sara Myers, Abe Klitzman, Jacob Myers, Mrs. Rosen, and Abe Rosen (Mrs. Rosen's husband). The child in the front is the Myers' daughter. The photograph was taken by Steele's Photographic Service of Belmar. (Sandra Epstein.)

After having a temporary home, the Presbyterian church received two lots from the Ocean Beach Association at Ninth and E Streets. The new building, as shown on this *c.* 1910 postcard, was dedicated in 1883.

The Congregation Sons of Israel Temple is one of the oldest synagogues in Monmouth County. Built in 1908, the temple (shown here in about 1910) continues today. Next door is a community building erected in the 1930s that is presently a yeshiva school. (Belmar Public Library.)

This notice of a gospel meeting from 1916 includes a picture of the Baptist church at the corner of Twelfth Avenue and F Street. It was moved to the corner of Thirteenth Avenue and E Street in 1925 and became the Calvary Baptist Church. (Collection of Dennis Lewis.)

Belmar's First Baptist Church began in July 1889 when services were temporarily conducted in Hoylers Hall on Tenth Avenue until the church was built in 1906. This is a modern photograph of the church, which is on Ninth Avenue.

circa 1914

The Methodist Episcopal church, organized in Ocean Beach in 1873, was the first church in the town, located at Tenth Avenue and D Street. In 1903, the church that is depicted on this 1912 postcard at Seventh Avenue and D Street was opened. Today's church is known as the First United Methodist Church.

1914

ST. ROSE CATHOLIC CHURCH,
BELMAR, N J

The St. Rose Roman Catholic Church, first organized in 1888 as a mission, held services in a rented building on Second Avenue. The present church on Seventh Avenue was erected in 1906. (Belmar Public Library.)

The St. Rose School eighth-grade class of 1948 stands on the steps of the old red brick school at Eighth Avenue and E Street, the girls with corsages and the boys with boutonnieres. The grammar school opened in 1921 and the high school in 1923. (Pat McCann Jr.)

The annual Vic Hirsch Trophy is being presented to Pat McCann Jr. in 1951. From left to right are Monsignor Peter J. Teston, Jack Kennedy, Coach Vic Hirsch, Pat McCann Jr., Commissioner John Ferruggiaro, and Father George Everett. (Pat McCann Jr.)

This was the first safety patrol at St. Rose School, c. 1956. From left to right are (first row) first three are unknown, F. McGovern, J. Remy, unknown, Thomas Nash, and Donald Nash; (middle row) unknown, John Rosenfeld, unknown, James Ferruggiaro, John Byrne, Francis Faas, unknown, and Paul Caverly; (back row) unknown, Patrolman Robert V. Pringle, Nick Carcich, Sister Mary Lupita, Larry Perone, Father Peter J. Teston, Peter Smith, Mother Joseph Bernard, George Geresi, Virgil Pierce, Police Chief Isola, and William Byrne. (Robert V. Pringle.)

In this photograph, also taken c. 1956, the smiling safety patrol of St. Rose School shows off the raincoats that were donated to them by Keystone Auto Club. (Robert V. Pringle.)

Pictured at the marina in August 1964 during Belmar's celebration of the New Jersey Tercentenary Festival, are, from left to right, Chairman Abraham Klitzman, Mildred Desmond Day (representing the Belmar Woman's Club), Secretary Elvin Simmill, and Guest Speaker Don Sterner. (Mildred Desmond Day.)

The weather must have been getting cold, judging from the clothing worn for this 1942 snapshot of year-round Belmarians Mildred Desmond (Day), who loaned this photograph, and her children. Delores Desmond (now McDermott) is to the left next to her sister, Patricia Desmond (now Daly), and little brother "Jimmy."

The Belmar St. Patrick's Day Parade, started in the early 1970s, may be the largest in the state. You are sure to find traditional bagpipers in every parade. Pictured above is a scene from the 1976 parade, in the year of the country's bicentennial.

In the 1976 St. Patrick's Day parade, the Irish-American float carrying beauty queens and sponsored by the Jerry Lynch Social and Athletic Club dazzles the spectators who are lined up on the sidewalk.

118

Pat McCann Jr. proudly escorts his mother, Kathleen McCann, deputy grand marshal of the 1976 Belmar St. Patrick's Day Parade. (Pat McCann Jr.)

Little Billy Sullivan and pretty "Colleen" charm the crowds at the 1976 Belmar St. Patrick's Day Parade.

The next volume of *Belmar* will include more about Belmar and its people in recent years. The St. Patrick's Day parade is already part of Belmar's history. The parade that began in 1973 will celebrate its 25th anniversary in 1998. Pictured above at the 1990 parade are, from left to right, Andrew Gallagher, Congressman Frank Pallone Jr., and Gerald Lynch (founder of the event). (Lois Gallagher.)

One of the few recent pictures in this volume, a photograph from May 17, 1997, is included because it relates directly to the history of Belmar—this image features the town's 125th birthday celebration. Mayor Kenneth Pringle and Mildred Desmond Day proudly cut the cake that was donated by Freedman's bakery. Standing next to Mrs. Day is Pat O'Keefe of the Belmar Tourism Development Commission.

Eight

By the Shores of Silver Lake

The image of Victorian buildings is reflected beautifully in the calm water of Silver Lake c. 1925. The building with two towers was the Brunswick Hotel. (Belmar Public Library.)

The Silver Lake Water Carnival was a "grand event" according to the writer of this postcard dated 1908. Festivals were held for many years, and today popular events such as Belmar's annual seafood festival are held in this area. (Moss Archives.)

This view of Silver Lake from the beach in the area of the Fifth Avenue Pavilion—which was then Gordon's—dates to 1908. The park area where the Huisman Gazebo stands today was still nothing but sand dunes then. (Collection of John Walsifer.)

Silver Lake, originally called West's Pond, lies wholly within the boundaries of Belmar. This postcard from 1910 shows the view from the north side at Eighth Avenue before part of the lake was filled in. Ferruggiaro Park now occupies part of this area. (Collection of John Walsifer.)

The house that was at 319 Eighth Avenue was the Werenburg Cottage, built in the early days of Belmar. When this photograph was taken c. 1890s, Silver Lake came right up to Eighth Avenue as shown here, before the north end of the lake was filled in. The house was torn down and a new house built on the site. (Robert V. and Lorraine Pringle.)

The Fifth Avenue Pavilion, flowerbeds, and fountain in front of Silver Lake are the subject of this linen postcard from the 1940s. The pavilion burned down in 1972, but was soon replaced. The current pavilion is named the John A. Taylor Pavilion in honor of the former mayor and well-respected citizen of Belmar.

In this popular linen postcard dated 1953, the bathing beauties may distract from the beauty of the "Belmar" flowerbed at Silver Lake.

The water from Silver Lake extended almost to the houses on Fifth Avenue after the devastating Hurricane of 1944. (Collection of John Walsifer.)

A 1960 postcard shows the park in front of Silver Lake and the fountain with a statue of a little girl and boy under an umbrella. The flowery "Belmar" was a well-known landmark for many years. (Collection of John Walsifer.)

The Campbell-Evans Hotel at 112 Fifth Avenue on the north side of Silver Lake, seen here as it looked in the 1940s, is now the Barclay Hotel. (Collection of Dennis Lewis.)

5th Avenue East from B Street, Belmar, N. J.

A popular postcard from the early twentieth century shows the houses that were on Fifth Avenue east from B Street, all with views of Silver Lake.

This postcard of children feeding swans at Silver Lake is postmarked 1931. Today, the Borough of Belmar discourages this activity because, among other things, feeding them keep them from migrating as they should, and may increase their susceptibility to disease.

A 1960s view shows children feeding ducks at the north end of Silver Lake. The island in the lake that can be seen here is man-made, originally built to provide a winter home for the birds. Today, the birds are encouraged to migrate. Although feeding the birds is not allowed today for environmental reasons, simply observing their beauty provides enjoyment for both children and adults.

Why did these swans cross the road in the early 1920s? The answer is to get to the other side, of course! Birds crossing the streets around Silver Lake are still a frequent sight in Belmar and drivers gladly wait for their feathered friends. (Belmar Public Library.)

Belmar is famous for the graceful swans of Silver Lake, said to be the first flock bred in America. This photograph is from about 1920. A swan appears on the crest of Belmar's official coat of arms. The swan provides a tranquil finale to this book, but a second volume may be in store as there is so much more about Belmar's past to be documented and enjoyed. (Belmar Public Library.)